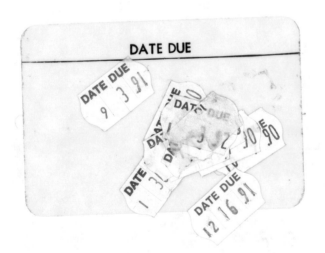

DATE DUE

An A·B·C of
Fashionable Animals

by
Cooper Edens
Alexandra Day
Welleran Poltarnees

GREEN TIGER PRESS, INC.
San Diego
1989

The Green Tiger Press, Inc., San Diego, California
First Edition
ISBN 0-88138-122-5
Manufactured in Hong Kong

2 4 6 8 10 9 7 5 3

Words for Adults

Someday, when I am old and have nothing to do but read and look at pictures, I will finish my magnum opus, on which I have been at work for 20 years, *The Encyclopedia of Dressed Animals*. There I will present all the species in their sartorial splendor. In the meantime I here show a few of my favorites, and raise some of the issues which *The Encyclopedia* will explore.

Why do animals delight us so much? Why are children so drawn to them? Is it, in part, because children need someone to pity, somewhere to lavish their parental impulses? Why do children's books so often put human clothes on the animals, and make them do human tasks in human environments? Perhaps it is really boys and girls, men and women, that the stories concern, and that we find the lessons more palatable when the characters are disguised as animals.

Whatever the answers to these questions, it is apparent that clothed animals often bring the best out of book illustrators, and for the readers are a boundless source of delight.

Welleran Poltarnees

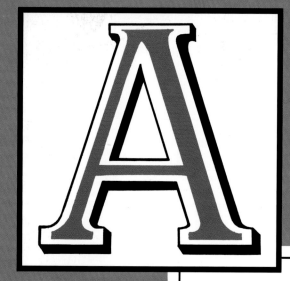

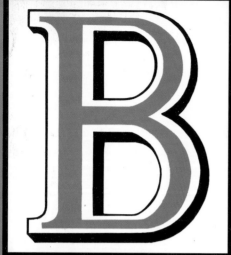

bear

cat

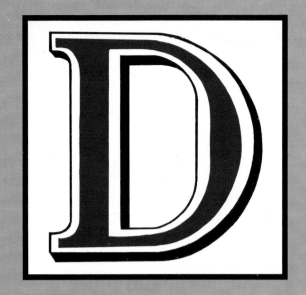

dog

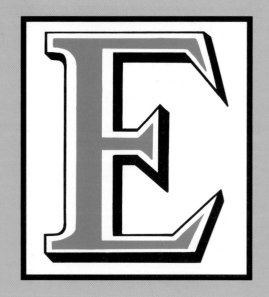

elephant

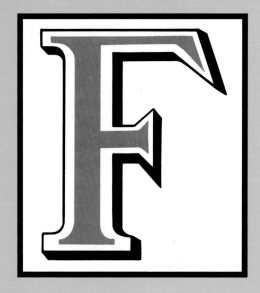

frog

G

giraffe

H

hippopotamus

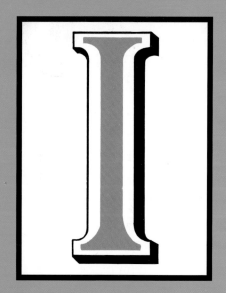

ibex

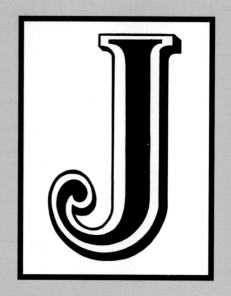

jaguar

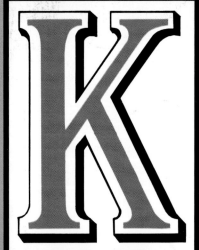

koala

L

lion

M

mouse

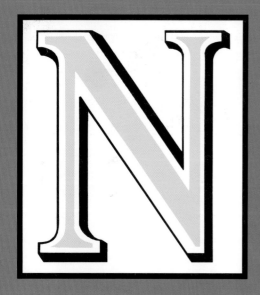

nightingale

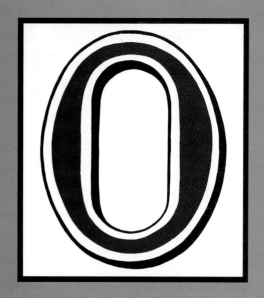

owl

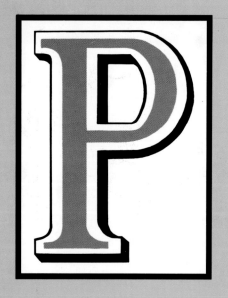

pig

quail

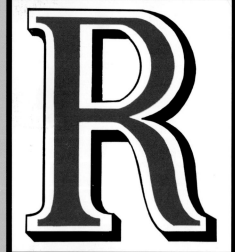

rabbit

S

squirrel

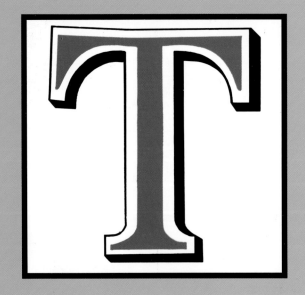

turkey

U

umbrella bird

V

vulture

W

Text on hat: WILLIE SHEPHE
OF THE SHEE

wolf

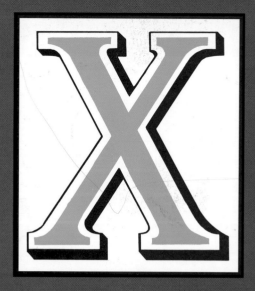

xiphias

yak

zebra

FATHER.

Picture Credits

Page

Front Cover   Anonymous, n.d.
Endpapers   Ludwig Bechstein, *Brüllaria*, 1893
Frontispiece   *The Roosevelt Bears Abroad*
Title Page   Cecil Aldin, *Cecil Aldin's Merry Party*, 1913
Copyright Page   Harry Neilson, *The Jungle School*, 1900
A   Harry Neilson, *The Jungle School*, 1900
A   L.J. Bridgman, *Bumps and Thumps*, 1903
B   V. Floyd Campbell, *The Traveling Bears in Outdoor Sports*, 1915
B   G.H.T., *Nister's Holiday Annual*, 1907
C   W.E. Hill, *Among Us Cats*, 1926
C   Louis Wain, *Louis Wain's Annual*, 1913
D   M. Coolidge, n.d.
D   Fritz Baumgarten, *Der Hunderzirkus*, n.d.
E   L. Leslie Brooke, *The Nursery Rhyme Book*, 1897
E   Harry Neilson, *More Jumbo Stories*, n.d.
F   Paul Woodroffe, *Thirty Old-Time Nursery Songs*, 1907
F   Peter Newell, *Mother Goose's Menagerie*, 1901
G   G.H. Thomas, *The Animal's Trip to Sea*, n.d.
G   N. Parker, *The Lays of the Grays*, n.d.
H   Anonymous, *The Story Book for Young Folks*, n.d.
H   J.J. Grandville, *Scènes de la Vie Privée et Publique des Animaux*, 1842
I   Harrison Cady, *St. Nicholas*, 1906
I   Harry Neilson, *An Animal A.B.C.*, 1901
J   Harrison Cady, *St. Nicholas*, 1906
J   Harry Neilson, *An Animal A.B.C.*, 1901
K   Norman Lindsay, *The Magic Pudding*, 1918
K   May Gibbs, *Mr. and Mrs. Bear and Friends*, 1943
L   W. Foster, *Nothing But Fun*, n.d.
L   L. Leslie Brooke, *Johnny Crow's Garden*, 1903
M   M. Bowley, *Father Tuck's Annual*, n.d.
M   Milo Winter, magazine illustration, n.d.
N   Albertine Randall Wheelan, *St. Nicholas*, 1916
N   J.J. Grandville, *Scènes de la Vie Privée et Publique des Animaux*, 1842